PEARSON PUBLISHING

Life in Tudor Times

Stewart Ross

Illustrations by Julie Beer

ISBN 1 85749 232 3

Published Pearson Publishing, Chesterton Mill, French's Road, Cambridge CB4 3NP

First edition 1995

Reprinted 1997

Text © Stewart Ross, 1995

Contents

The Tudors

Who were the Tudors?

The Tudors were a family.

For over 100 years they were the most important family in England.

Many of them were kings and queens, or **monarchs**. When a country has a king or queen we call it a monarchy.

Queen Elizabeth, one of the most famous Tudor monarchs

What did the Tudors do?

There were Tudor monarchs from 1485 to 1603.

In those days English monarchs were much more important than they are today. They were in charge of the **government** of the country – they made decisions on matters such as spending money and defending England against attackers. Monarchs who govern are known as **rulers**.

Of course the Tudor monarchs could not govern by themselves. They chose a **council** to help them.

If they were sensible, they also listened to the talk going on in **parliament**. Men came to parliament from all over the country to discuss new laws and to let the monarch know what they were thinking.

The Tudor family

The Tudor family once lived in Wales.

- In 1485 Henry Tudor came to England and became king. He was the seventh king of England named Henry, so we call him Henry the Seventh. This is usually written: **Henry VII**.
  Henry became king in 1485 and died in 1509, so we say he **reigned** from 1485 to 1509.
- Henry VII was **succeeded** by his son, another Henry. He is known as Henry the Eighth, or **Henry VIII**.
- In 1547 Henry VIII died and his son Edward Tudor became **King Edward VI**. Edward reigned for only six years.
- Edward had no children. In 1553 he was succeeded by his sister Mary, **Mary I**.
- The last Tudor monarch was Mary's sister, Elizabeth. **Elizabeth I** did not marry and had no children. When she died in 1603 the line of Tudor monarchs came to an end.

We can write the Tudor monarchs like this:

Name	Dates of reign
Henry VIII ᵥᵢᵢ	1485-1509
Henry VIII	1509-1547
Edward VI	1547-1553
Mary I	1553-1558
Elizabeth I	1558-1603

Or we can draw a family diagram, called a **family tree**:

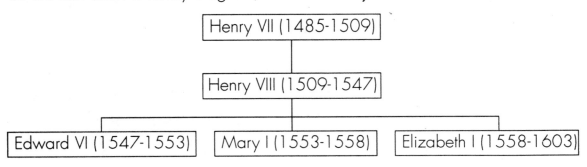

Something to do

1 Copy out the Tudor family tree. Using this book, trace or draw pictures of the monarchs and stick them on the tree next to their names.

2 Make a family tree of your own family. How far back can you go?

King Henry VII

Childhood

Henry Tudor was born in Pembroke Castle on 28 January 1457.

His mother, Margaret, was only 13-years-old. Edmund Tudor, his father, had died two and a half months before. Edmund had been Earl of Richmond. The baby Henry now **inherited** his father's title – he became Earl of Richmond.

Danger!

Two powerful families, **York** and **Lancaster**, were fighting for the English throne. The Lancasters were Henry Tudor's relatives.

York beat Lancaster, and Edward of York became king.

The 14-year-old Henry Tudor was now the Lancastrian **heir** to the throne. The Lancastrians were afraid that the Yorkists might try to kill Henry, so his Uncle Jasper took him to Brittany in France. Here he was safe.

Henry VII, the first Tudor monarch

Henry becomes king

In 1485, when he was 28, Henry came to England with an army and won the crown. This is explained on pages 23 to 24.

He ended the squabble between York and Lancaster by marrying Elizabeth, a Yorkist princess. Henry was a strong, careful king who left his kingdom in good order for his son, Henry VIII.

King Henry VIII

The selfish hero

Henry VIII is one of the most famous English monarchs. He was eighteen when he became king on the death of his father.

In some ways Henry was a hero – he was tall, handsome and good at many things, such as sport and music. But he was also spoilt and selfish. He always wanted his own way and was cruel to those who opposed him.

Henry VIII as a young man

War and wives

Henry went to war several times. He spent a lot of money on the army and navy, but his wars were not very successful.

Henry relied on **ministers**, such as Cardinal Wolsey and Thomas Cromwell, to do much of the hard work. When things went wrong, he punished them severely – Thomas Cromwell was **beheaded** in 1540.

Henry married six times. His wives were Catherine of Aragon, Anne Boleyn, Jane Seymour, Anne of Cleves, Catherine Howard and Catherine Parr. He divorced Catherine of Aragon and Anne of Cleves and beheaded Anne Boleyn and Catherine Howard. The story of his first two wives is told on pages 25 and 26.

By the end of his life Henry was overweight, ill and very bad tempered. Most English were rather relieved when he finally died in 1547.

King Edward VI

The boy king

Edward Tudor was the son of Henry VIII and Jane Seymour. She died shortly after Edward was born.

Although Edward's sisters Mary and Elizabeth were older than him, the law said that he should be monarch before them because he was male. He was only ten years old when he became king.

A short reign

Edward was too young to rule on his own. The government was managed for him by the Duke of Somerset, then by the Duke of Northumberland.

Edward was never very healthy and he died in 1553, aged 15.

Edward VI, the boy king

What can you remember?

Fill in the gaps in these sentences with the right words from the following list:

Jane Seymour   1509   Tudor   Thomas Cromwell   1547

1 Henry VIII died in _____.

2 Edward VI's family name was _____.

3 The minister _____ was executed in 1540.

4 _____ was Henry VIII's third wife.

Something to do

Colour in the pictures of the first three Tudor monarchs and write underneath the dates of their reigns.

Queen Mary I

Catherine's daughter

Mary was the daughter of Henry VIII's first wife, the Spanish princess Catherine. When Mary was 17, Henry divorced her mother and Mary was in disgrace.

Henry also ordered changes to England's religion, but Mary and her mother stuck to the old, **Roman Catholic** ways. (You can find out more about this on pages 25 to 28.)

Queen Mary I, who was nicknamed 'Bloody Mary'

A short, sad reign

When her brother Edward died in 1553, Mary became queen. She was determined to bring back her mother's Roman Catholicism.

About 300 men who refused to change were **executed** by being burned alive. This made Mary unpopular and she was given the nickname 'Bloody Mary'.

Mary's Spanish husband Philip was unpopular, too. Finally, Mary went to war with France and was defeated.

Few tears were shed when she died in 1558. (There is more about Mary on pages 27 and 28.)

Something to do

Look up the meaning of the word **martyr** and explain it in your own words.

Queen Elizabeth I

Problems, problems, problems!

Anne Boleyn, Elizabeth's mother, was beheaded when Elizabeth was only two years old.

Life was difficult for the princess during the reigns of her father, brother and sister, and when she became queen herself she faced many problems.

- She had to sort out the country's religion.
- She was short of money.
- She did not know whom to marry.
- She had to decide England's **foreign policy** – how it was to get on with other countries.

Elizabeth the Great?

Elizabeth was tall, quite good-looking, intelligent, tough and knew exactly how to behave as a queen. She ruled better than most people expected. She was lucky and chose able ministers. She also lived long enough for people to get used to her ways.

- She sorted out religion by setting up a new Church of England.
- She was very careful with money, although she always complained that she did not have enough.
- She never married.
- She avoided war as long as she could. Fortunately, when war came, her soldiers and sailors were quite successful. (The story of the famous Spanish Armada is on page 30.)

Because she managed so well, some people call the queen 'Elizabeth the Great'. There is a picture of Queen Elizabeth on page 3.

What can you remember?

Put a tick (✔) in the box if the sentence is correct:

1 Elizabeth married a Spanish prince. ☐

2 Mary was a Roman Catholic. ☐

3 Foreign policy is how a country gets on with other countries. ☐

4 About 300 martyrs were executed in Mary's reign. ☐

5 Elizabeth avoided war for as long as she could. ☐

Something to do

1 Draw a picture of something that interests you from the reign of *either* Mary *or* Elizabeth.

2 Write a few sentences on 'My favourite Tudor .

Sources

How do we find out about the Tudors?

We find out about Tudor times from **sources**, or **evidence**. A source is anything which tells us about the past.

Sources are clues or evidence about the past. Historians use sources like detectives. They put together all the evidence to build up a picture of the past. Beware! Sources do not always agree with each other.

Types of source

The best sources come from the time we want to know about. They include:

1   Things written in the past, such as letters, diaries or books.

2   Paintings, drawings, carvings, photographs and films.

3   Anything people made or built in the past – from cathedrals to cooking pots.

4   The spoken word, *either* recorded *or* said by people who were alive at the time. (We have no recordings from Tudor times!)

Other sources are usually books written by people who have studied original sources. They are a quick and easy way of finding out about the past.

Something to do

1   Study this picture carefully. What might you learn about Tudor times by looking at this picture?

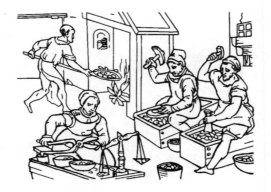

Minting coins in Tudor times

2   Write down six sources which tell us about Tudor England.

Measuring time

When did it happen?

We measure the time each day in seconds, minutes and hours. 24 hours make a day. Except in leap years, 365 days make a year. Days and years are measured in **dates**.

AD and BC

We arrange dates from the birth of Jesus Christ. The first year of his life we call the year 1 **AD**. The second year was year 2 AD, and so on.

If it is clear what we are talking about, we do not need to write AD. For example, 1547 (when Henry VII died) was one thousand, five hundred and forty-seven years after Jesus' birth.

Dates before the year of Jesus' birth are known as **BC**. They are counted *backwards* from the time of Christ. For example, 1500 BC came before 300 BC.

Centuries

A **century** is 100 years. We number centuries, like dates, from the birth of Jesus Christ.

The first century AD went from 1 AD to 100 AD. We are now living in the **20th century** (1901-2000). The Tudor monarchs lived mostly in the **sixteenth century** (1501-1600).

Something to do

1 What is the exact *date* and *time* at this moment? _____

_____

2 What was the number of the last century? _____

3 When did the tenth century begin _____ and end? _____

4 In which century was: a Henry VII born? _____

b Queen Elizabeth I born? _____

The royal court

What was the court?

The royal **court** was the king or queen's household – the buildings as well as the people in it. The court was always full of servants, ministers and visitors from England and overseas.

Because monarchs were so powerful, the court was the most important place in the whole country.

The court of Henry VIII

What happened at court?

Two sorts of things went on at court, usually at the same time:

i   The court was a place of entertainment. Monarchs liked to live in great style. They held dances, feasts, concerts, plays and many other entertainments for the **courtiers** who were with them.
ii The court was also a place where people came to get things done. Some came to discuss government with the monarch. Others came asking for favours, for money or for a job. There was never enough for everyone.

With so many people trying to get what they could, court was not always a very pleasant place.

Court life

The Tudor court was as busy as a beehive. The monarch and their family were looked after by hundreds of servants.

At the centre was the **privy chamber**. Here a king was helped in matters such as getting dressed, by **gentlemen of the bedchamber**. A queen had **ladies-in-waiting**.

The rest of the court was looked after by the **Lord Chamberlain** and **Lord Steward**. There were secretaries to take care of the paperwork, **treasurers** to manage the money, guards, musicians, doctors, **chaplains**, cooks, gardeners, maids and an assortment of other servants.

Elizabeth I with some of her courtiers

What can you remember?

Fill in the gaps in these sentences with the right words from the following list:

      court   chaplain   privy chamber   ladies-in-waiting

1 In private a queen was looked after by her _____.

2 A monarch and their household was the centre of the _____.

3 The _____ was the most private part of the court.

4 A royal _____ looked after religious services at court.

Something to do

Colour in the picture above and, on a separate piece of paper, list the enjoyable things about life at court.

Palaces and travels

Court on the move

The Tudor monarchs did not usually stay in one place for long. They travelled around the country. Where they went, courtiers came too.

They moved about because:
- palaces became very dirty when they were full of people. When the monarch was out of the way, servants gave the place a good clean
- monarchs became bored with staying in one place
- the Tudors wanted to see and be seen by their people. A visit reminded people how grand the king or queen was and gave the monarch a chance to keep an eye on things.

Henry VIII sailing for France, 1532

A mixed blessing

Henry VII and the young Edward VI travelled a good deal. Henry VIII was not keen on going north. Elizabeth made summer **progresses**, but spent most of the time around London and Windsor.

People had mixed feelings when they heard the monarch was coming to their part of the country.

A royal visit was a great honour and might lead to favours for them. But it was also very expensive. The monarch would expect presents and the courtiers might eat their hosts out of house and home!

Palaces

Sometimes the Tudor monarchs stayed in the mansions of the rich and powerful. Normally, however, they lived in one of their own palaces.

There were many royal palaces. Some, such as Westminster in London, the monarchs **inherited** from previous monarchs; others they bought or just took. Between 1535 and 1547 Henry VIII took about 30 palaces from the church!

The great Tudor palace at Hampton Court

Inside the palace

Although each royal palace was different, most of them had similar types of rooms.

The biggest was the hall, a huge room for **banquets**. The monarch sat at the top table on a raised platform. At the opposite end there was often a **gallery** where musicians played.

Monarchs had their own private rooms or **chambers**, with a huge four-poster bed in the bed chamber. Courtiers were received by the monarch in an **audience chamber**. The walls of the main rooms were decorated with huge **tapestries**. Paintings hung in a long gallery. Huge open fires provided warmth.

The servants shared bedrooms, known as their **quarters**. These were sometimes in the attic where it was cold in winter and very hot in the summer.

There was no electricity, gas or running water. At night time hundreds of candles provided light. This made the rooms stuffy and smoky. The lavatories were just buckets which the servants had to empty every day. You can imagine how smelly a palace became when the court had been there for several weeks!

The cost of living

Most Tudor palaces were very grand. They had dozens of rooms and were surrounded by huge gardens and parks.

This meant that they were very expensive to maintain. By Elizabeth's time there was not enough money to look after them all. Some fell into ruin, others were sold.

The favourite ones remained, however. They were all in the south:
- In London: Whitehall and St James's.
- Beside the Thames: Windsor, Greenwich, Richmond and Hampton Court.
- In Surrey: Nonsuch, Oatlands.

What can you remember?

1 Which were the Tudors' favourite London palaces? _____ and
   _____.

2 In which room were banquets held? _____.

3 What were Elizabeth's summer travels called?_____.

4 Why did the Tudor monarchs travel round the country?

   _____

   _____

5 What were the servants' rooms called? _____

6 What kind of bed did a Tudor monarch sleep in? _____

Something to do

1 Colour the picture on page 16.

2 Imagine Henry VIII is coming to stay in your mansion. Write a letter to your brother saying why you are pleased and worried by this news.

Clothes

Looking your best

It was important for courtiers always to look their best. In Tudor times, those who could afford it wore amazing clothes – brightly coloured, rich and often decorated with jewels.

As there were no man-made materials in the sixteenth century. Clothes were made from wool, linen, silk and other natural fibres.

Women's dresses were long, tightly fitted at the waist, with **ruffs** at the wrist and neck. The sleeves were heavily decorated. Men wore a tight type of jacket, known as a **doublet**, which also had ruffs. Below the waist they wore puffed out **breeches** and **hose** (tights) on their legs.

Men and women generally wore hats.

A man and woman in court dress of the Tudor period

Something to do

1 Colour the picture and label these items: ruff, hose, breeches, jewels, doublet.

2 Design and draw your own Tudor outfit for a man or woman.

Royal entertainment

Music and dancing

The Tudors were quite a musical family, particularly Henry VIII and Elizabeth. Henry had music wherever he went, even when he went to war. His royal choir was excellent and he sang well himself. He collected instruments, too, playing the lute, organ and **virginals**.

Music was also important at Elizabeth's court. She played the virginals, but not as well as her father.

Dancing was popular at court. It was nothing like a disco! The dances were complicated and dancing men and women did not get close together.

A court picnic

Hunting

Hunting was more dangerous and bloodthirsty than it is today. Henry VIII loved it. The part of modern London known as the Isle of Dogs is named after the place where he kept his hounds.

The huntsmen chased deer, not foxes. All day they careered around the royal forests on horseback, horns blaring, dogs barking and men shouting. In a single day's hunting Henry tired out eight or ten horses.

Other entertainment

The Tudor monarchs arranged all sorts of other things to amuse themselves and their courtiers.

Indoors there were plays, betting games, and a host of entertainers, such as jugglers, acrobats and **jesters**.

Outdoors there was archery, tennis, athletics and, above all, **tournaments**. By the time of Henry VIII these were beginning to go out of fashion, but as a young man the king adored them and was always winning prizes. He could throw a spear as far as anyone and was champion with the two-handed sword.

Nonsuch Palace, where Henry spent many busy days enjoying himself

What can you remember?

Put a tick (✔) in the box if the sentence is correct:

1 A doublet is a sort of jacket. ☐

2 Tudor dancing was like a modern disco. ☐

3 Tudor monarchs hunted foxes. ☐

4 Queen Elizabeth played the virginals. ☐

Something to do

1 Draw your own picture of a Tudor hunt, dance or tournament

2 Write a description of your favourite Tudor court entertainment.

Famous courtiers

Catherine Howard

Catherine Howard first came to the court of Henry VIII in the autumn of 1539. The king was about to be married to his fourth wife, the foreign princess Anne of Cleves. Catherine was to be one of the new queen's ladies-in-waiting.

Catherine was a lively and attractive 19-year-old who knew how to handle men. Henry – 49 and bad-tempered – immediately fell for her. He watched her, he showed off before her, he gave her presents. She danced before him and flirted quite openly. Londoners began to gossip about how often Henry crossed the Thames to where Catherine lived.

Henry VIII as an old man

In January 1540 Henry went ahead with his marriage to Anne of Cleves. Poor Anne! Her new husband was crazy about the bright girl at his court. He divorced Anne in early July and married Catherine 18 days later.

The marriage was a disaster. Catherine had no love for her grumpy, middle-aged husband. She soon started seeing an old boyfriend, Francis Dereham, and the handsome courtier, Thomas Culpepper.

Henry was bound to find out. When he did, towards the end of 1541, he was furious, then miserable. But for Catherine there was no escape. She and her two boyfriends were executed. Courtiers said the king was almost mad with unhappiness.

The Earl of Leicester

When Elizabeth Tudor became queen of England in 1558, all her subjects were asking the same question – whom would she marry? She was 25, intelligent and good looking. She would have no trouble finding a husband.

But it was not that easy. The man she loved and wanted to marry was a tall and attractive courtier named Robert Dudley. But Dudley was married.

Elizabeth made her friend Master of the Horse. Rumours spread about the couple. Then something terrible happened. Dudley's wife Amy was found dead at the bottom of the stairs. Her neck was broken.

Robert Dudley, Earl of Leicester

Amy's death was a tragic accident – she had simply fallen down the stairs. But people began to gossip even more. Was it really an accident? they whispered. Perhaps Dudley had arranged for Amy to be killed so that he could marry the queen?

It was a very dangerous time for Elizabeth. In the end, she decided to put her country before her heart. Marrying Dudley would make people jealous of him. Besides, she did not wish to share her power with anyone. She would not marry.

The queen and the handsome courtier remained the best of friends. He stayed at court and was made Earl of Leicester. Fifteen years later he remarried. Elizabeth was furious, but she forgave him. Perhaps secretly she still loved him?

Henry VII and Richard III

The ambitious duke

Richard Duke of York was **ambitious**. During the reign of his brother, King Edward IV, Richard made a name for himself as a soldier. In 1483, while fighting in Scotland, he learned that Edward had died and his 13-year-old son was now King Edward V.

Richard hurried back to London. He got rid of his enemies and put the young king and his brother in the Tower of London. There, he said, they would be safe.

The parliament now asked Richard to be king, and he was crowned as King Richard III on 6 July 1483. He had achieved his highest ambition.

King Richard III, the last monarch from the House of York

The ruthless king

Richard turned out to be a very capable monarch who ruled with considerable skill. But he was also **ruthless** – he would stop at nothing to get what he wanted.

Some of the most powerful men in the kingdom were suspicious of the way he had seized the crown. They also wanted to know what had happened to the princes in the Tower of London. The boys had not been seen for a long time and it was whispered that Richard had paid someone to kill them.

Sooner or later there was going to be a **rebellion**.

The Lancastrians

The first rebellion was led by Richard's old friend and **ally**, the Duke of Buckingham. The revolt failed and Buckingham was executed.

All eyes now turned to the leader of the House of Lancaster, Henry Tudor, Earl of Richmond. (We first met Henry on page 5.) Supporters of the Lancastrians believed that Henry, not Richard, should be king. For his safety, at the time Henry was living in Brittany, France.

A soldier in armour at the time of Richard III

Bosworth

As Richard became more unpopular with the **nobles**, Henry saw his chance. He gathered his supporters and sailed to Milford Haven, landing on 1 August 1485. King Richard collected an army and marched to meet the invader.

The two armies met at Bosworth Field in Leicestershire. Here they fought a bloody battle. Some of the king's supporters broke their promise to help him and Richard's army was defeated. Richard died fighting.

Henry claimed the crown, calling himself Henry VII. The time of the Tudors had begun.

What can you remember?

1 Where did Richard of York and Henry Tudor fight a battle? _____

2 Give the dates of the reign of Richard III: _____

Henry VIII, wives and the pope

Henry VIII and Queen Catherine

Henry VIII married Catherine of Aragon from Spain soon after becoming King.

In those days monarchs did not marry for love. They usually married an important person chosen by their parents. Princess Catherine had been chosen by Henry's father because England and Spain had an **alliance** with each other.

Henry and Catherine got on quite well for a time, and in 1516 they had a daughter, Mary. But Henry wanted a son to become king when he died. After 20 years of marriage it was clear that Catherine was not going to have a son.

Queen Catherine of Aragon

Divorce?

Henry began to think about ending his marriage with Queen Catherine. He wanted a divorce so that he could marry someone else.

At that time the only religion allowed in England was Roman Catholicism. The head of the Roman Catholics was the pope, who lived in Rome. Only the pope could give Henry permission for a divorce. But he wouldn't do so.

Henry's answer

Henry and some of his ministers decided to form their own **church**. They got parliament to help them.

Parliament made new laws (called **acts**) that set up the **Church of England**. The Christian religion of the new church was quite like Roman Catholicism, except that the king was head of the Church of England, not the pope.

Henry was now able to divorce Catherine and marry his girlfriend, Anne Boleyn.

Queen Anne had a daughter, Elizabeth. Three years later Henry had her head cut off. He said she was too friendly with other men.

Anne Boleyn, Henry VIII's second wife

What can you remember?

Tick (✔) the **three** things that happened in the reign of Henry VIII:

1 Henry married Mary.

2 England became a Roman Catholic country.

3 Henry married Anne Boleyn.

4 Edward VI changed the Church of England.

5 The Church of England was set up.

6 Parliament **passed** some new acts about religion.

Something to do

Tell the story of Henry VIII and Anne Boleyn, using your own words and pictures.

Queen Mary and Lady Jane Grey

Henry VII's children

Henry VII had four children:
- Prince Arthur, who died in 1502
- Henry, who became King Henry VIII
- Margaret, who married King James V of Scotland
- Mary, who married twice. Her first husband was King Louis of France. Her second was Charles Brandon, Duke of Suffolk. Their daughter married Henry Grey.

Lady Jane Grey

During the reign of young Edward VI, England's Christian religion was changed from Roman Catholic to **Protestant**.

When Edward died in 1553, some Protestants did not want Mary to become queen because she was a Roman Catholic. They were afraid that she would try to get rid of Protestantism.

So in place of Mary Tudor they chose a Protestant queen. Her name was Lady Jane Grey, the great-granddaughter of Henry VII.

Lady Jane Grey, queen for ten days

In the Tower

Most English people did not want the **succession** changed. Whatever her religion, they wanted Mary to be queen because she was the elder daughter of Henry VIII.

As a result, Jane was queen for only 10 days. When Mary came to London huge crowds turned out to greet her.

The wretched Jane, who had never been very keen on being made queen, was locked in the Tower of London.

Rebellion and execution

Mary's popularity did not last. The following year there was a rebellion against her, led by Sir Thomas Wyatt and Jane's father. They did not want England to be Roman Catholic and they said Jane should be queen again.

Wyatt's forces reached London but could not cross the bridge into the city. Shortly afterwards Wyatt was captured by Queen Mary's soldiers.

The end came swiftly. Wyatt and 100 of his followers were executed. People dipped their handkerchiefs in his blood, believing he was a martyr. The following day, 12 February 1554, Lady Jane Grey was also beheaded.

What can you remember?

Put a tick (✔) in the box if the sentence is correct:

1 Lady Jane Grey never became queen. ☐

2 Edward VI and Mary I were children of Henry VIII. ☐

3 Lady Jane Grey was related to Henry VII. ☐

4 Lady Jane Grey was a Catholic and Mary Tudor was a Protestant. ☐

5 Some people thought Sir Thomas Wyatt was a martyr. ☐

6 Henry VII had three children. ☐

Something to do

1 Draw and label your own picture of any part of the life of Lady Jane Grey.

2 Explain in your own words why Lady Jane Grey was executed.

Elizabeth I and the Spanish Armada

Elizabeth I and Philip of Spain

Western Europe at the time of Elizabeth I

When Elizabeth became queen in 1558, Spain was the strongest country in Europe.

Queen Mary I had been married to King Philip of Spain, and England and Spain were friends. This friendship did not last. Here are some reasons why:

- England was Protestant, Spain was Roman Catholic. They did not trust each other, and Philip II wanted all Europe to be Roman Catholic.
- Spanish ships **traded** all over the world, especially in America. English sailors, like Sir Francis Drake, sometimes attacked Spanish ships. This annoyed Philip.
- English soldiers helped Dutch Protestants who were fighting a war with Spain.
- Elizabeth's Roman Catholic cousin, Mary Queen of Scots, said she ought to be queen of England instead of Elizabeth. In 1587 Elizabeth ordered Mary to be beheaded. Philip was furious.

War

The war between England and Spain began in 1585. They fought each other in the Netherlands, France, Ireland and at sea.

Philip decided to invade England. He collected an **armada** which set sail from Spain in May 1588.

The Spanish Armada

The battle between the British and Spanish ships took place in the Channel during July and August. It lasted for several weeks.

The Armada was damaged by English guns, **fireships** and storms. In the end it gave up and sailed home. Many of the ships were wrecked on the journey.

England was not a very powerful country at that time. The English were very proud at having defeated the Spanish Armada.

From a tapestry picture of the Spanish Armada

What can you remember?

Fill in the gaps in these sentences with the right words from the following list:

traded   Armada   invade

1 The Spanish _____ was made up of many ships.

2 Spanish sailors _____ all over the world.

3 Philip II tried to _____ England in 1588.

Something to do

Draw your own picture of English ships fighting the Spanish Armada. Underneath make a list of the reasons why the Spanish did not manage to conquer England.

Exploring

The world

Look carefully at these two maps of the world. The first was printed in 1482, just before Henry VII became king. The second was printed in 1570, 88 years later.

A map of the world, drawn in 1482

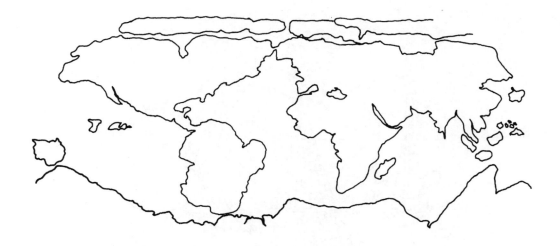

A map of the world, drawn in 1570

5 Sailors and Explorers

Something to do

1 Using a modern map of the world, draw the following: Italy, Ireland, North America, South America, Africa, India, China, Arabia and Australia.

2 Now draw them as they were shown on the two maps above. Don't worry if you can't find some places on the old maps.

3 Make lists of the places whose shape was not very well understood in:

a 1482 _____

b 1570 _____

Explorers

Old maps show us that by the end of the Tudor **era** people knew much more about the world than they had done a hundred years before.

The men who found out about the world were explorers. They travelled in wooden sailing ships, making long and dangerous voyages across the sea.

Explorers sailed west to North and South America, and east round Africa to India and the Far East. Two ships sailed right round the world for the first time.

Most of the explorers came from the countries of Western Europe. Look at a map of Europe and see if you can work out why this was.

The first explorers came from Portugal, Spain and Italy. Soon they were joined by men from England, France and the Netherlands.

From a sixteenth-century picture of an ocean-going vessel

Why did they go?

The explorers went on their voyages for many reasons.

- Most wanted to get rich.
- Some were looking for gold.
- Others were looking for valuable **cargoes** to bring back to home and sell. The sort of things they were looking for were silk, sugar and **spices**.
- Others went to tell people in distant lands about the Christian religion. They are known as **missionaries**.

Explorers thought they would find people like this in South America!

What can you remember?

Fill in the gaps in these sentences with the right words from the following list:

> missionaries   cargoes   era   voyages

1 European sailors made _____ across the seas to new lands.

2 The _____ wanted to tell other people about their religion.

3 Explorers were looking for valuable _____ to fill their ships.

4 There were many explorers in the Tudor _____ .

Something to do

1 Colour and label the picture on page 32.

2 Find the names of five famous explorers of this period. Write down where they came from, and when and where they went.

Sir Francis Drake

The sailor boy

Francis Drake was born in Devonshire in about 1540. He went to sea at the age of 13. To begin with he stayed in the waters around Britain, learning all about sailing and **navigation**. He learned how to fight, too.

When he was in his 20s he went on ships sailing down the coast of Africa and over to America, known as the **New World**.

Sir Francis Drake

Plunder and fame

In 1567 Drake sailed to the New World as captain of his own ship, the *Judith*. He met a Spanish fleet and was lucky to escape with his life.

In those days the Spanish claimed to own most of America, and they disliked ships from other nations going to trade there.

Drake went back to America three more times. This time his voyages were more successful. He became rich on the **plunder** which he brought home. As there was no war between England and Spain, the Spaniards called Drake a pirate. But the English thought he was a hero, so Queen Elizabeth did nothing about it.

Round the world

In 1577 Drake sailed right round South America and into the Pacific Ocean. He wanted to rob the Spanish **galleons** in the Pacific.

Drake attacked the Spaniards and stole their valuable cargoes. He then sailed right round the world back to England. His voyage had taken him almost three years. Queen Elizabeth made him a **knight** – *Sir* Francis Drake.

Sir Francis went on fighting the Spanish until he died in 1596.

A Spanish galleon

What can you remember?

Put a circle round the correct answer:

1 Drake's chief enemies were the: French   Spanish   Dutch

2 He lived during the reign of: Elizabeth I   Elizabeth II   Henry VIII

3 The ocean to the west of America is the: Atlantic   Pacific   Channel

4 When Francis Drake came home Elizabeth made him a: knight night pirate

Something to do

Imagine you are King Philip II of Spain. Write a letter to Queen Elizabeth in 1580 complaining about Francis Drake.

Sir Walter Raleigh

The man who did many things

Sir Walter Raleigh was another famous English explorer and adventurer. He was born in Devon in 1552 and died in 1618. We say his **dates** were 1552-1618.

He was famous for his many interests:

- As a young man he fought as a soldier in France.
- Like Drake, he also fought against the Spanish.
- He was one of Elizabeth's favourites. She gave him jobs that made him rich.
- He became a Member of Parliament.
- He was a writer, too.
- He was interested in **founding** English **colonies** – places in newly-discovered lands where English people could go to live. They were ruled by the queen, like England. He tried to found a colony in North America, called Virginia. But the **settlers** could not survive on their own.

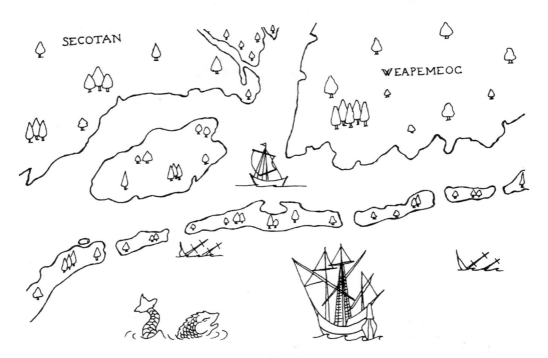

From an Elizabethan picture of the New World, 1585

Plots and problems

When Queen Elizabeth died in 1603, King James I from the Stuart family became king.

Sir Walter was arrested and locked in the Tower of London. It was said that he had plotted against the king. Sir Walter remained in the Tower for many years. While he was there he wrote a *History of the World.*

In 1616 James I let Raleigh out of the Tower. The explorer said he knew where to find gold in the New World. A year later he set sail for South America. He had fights with the Spanish and returned home without the gold he had promised.

King James wanted gold, but he did not want trouble with Spain. In 1618 Sir Walter was executed.

Sir Walter Raleigh

What can you remember?

1 Name the colony Sir Walter tried to found: _____

2 Where was Sir Walter between 1603 and 1616? _____

3 What are the dates of Sir Walter Raleigh? _____

4 Which king ordered Sir Walter to be executed? _____

Something to do

English settlers in North America often gave their towns and colonies English place names. Sometimes they put the word 'New' in front. New York is a good example. Try to find other place names like this on a map of the USA.

Towns

An empty land

Do you know how many people live in England today? More than 45 million!

When the first Tudor became king, the **population** of England was not much more than 2 million.

Most people were farmers, living in small villages. There were a lot more woods and empty spaces than today. The towns were small, too.

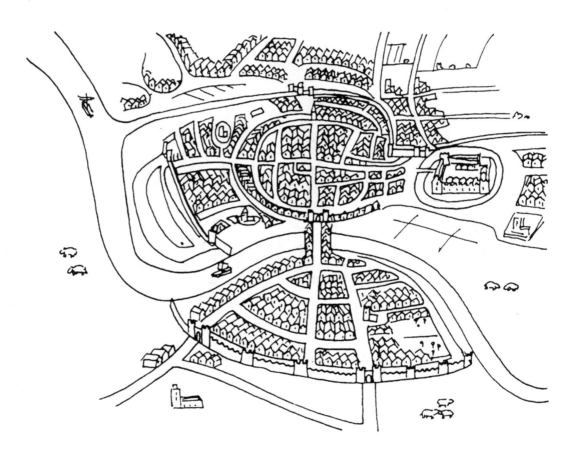

From a Tudor map of Bristol. The population was about 8000.
Today it is 500 000

Something to do

1 Colour the map of Bristol and label the river, the city wall, fields and two churches.

2 Explain how you can tell it is not a modern city.

A growing population

One of the biggest changes taking place in England during Tudor times was the growing size of the population.

When Elizabeth I died in 1601, the population of England had risen to about 4 million. This means that the population had doubled during Tudor times.

A street in a Tudor town

Town life

The centre of a Tudor town was the church or cathedral. Everybody had to go to religious services, so most towns had more than one church.

Another important place was the market, where goods and animals were sold on market day. People came into town from the villages on market day to do their shopping and business.

The shops were small, often with people living above them. There were no supermarkets. Each shop sold only one thing, such as shoes, cloth or bread. These were usually made at the back of the shop.

As there were no drains or water pipes in the houses, the streets quickly filled up with all sorts of rubbish.

Trade

England became a wealthier country in Tudor times. Much of the new wealth came from trade and **manufacture**. Thousands of new houses were built to make homes for the growing population.

English sheep produced very fine wool, which was **exported**. English **merchants** could be found in all the large cities of Europe.

Taking goods to market

At the same time, more and more English trading ships were sailing to different corners of the world. They imported the things which English people wanted from other countries, such as spices, wine, tobacco and sugar. They exported goods from England, particularly wool and cloth.

To help English merchants, parliament made laws saying that trade with England had to be carried out in English ships.

What can you remember?

Fill in the gaps in these sentences with the right words from the following list:

   population   imported   manufactured   merchants

1 In 1600 the _____ of England was about 4 million.

2 The English _____ sugar from other countries.

3 Cloth _____ from English wool was exported to many countries.

4 There were busy English _____ in most European cities.

The countryside

The poor

In Tudor times the rich people were very, very rich. They had huge houses, dozens of servants and did not need to work. But very few people lived like this – perhaps 1 in every 100, or 1 per cent.

Most men and women were dreadfully poor. If the weather was bad in the summer and the harvest was bad, there was not enough food and they starved.

The poor had wretched houses and tattered clothes. They were often ill and were lucky to live to the age of 30. To make matters worse, if they did not find work they could be punished. They were **flogged** and **branded** with the letter V for **vagrant**, meaning someone who was too lazy to work!

A beggar

At home

The houses of ordinary people were small and not very comfortable. They had no running water, no power and no lavatories. Cooking was done on open fires.

Few children went to school, most had to start work at an early age.

Can you imagine what your life would be like without TV, baths or electric light?

Village life

England was divided up into **counties** (sometimes called **shires**). Most of them (such as Yorkshire) still exist today. Each county was made up of many small **parishes**, each with a village and church.

Most people lived in these tiny villages and farmed the surrounding fields. Because there were no newspapers, TV or radio, they had little idea what the government was doing and they rarely saw the monarch. Their village and county were all-important to them. They thought of their county as their country.

Only the towns had shops. Many of the things which people needed for their everyday life were made in the village. Something special, like a new hat or ribbons, had to be bought from a **pedlar** or at the local market.

Making hay – in Tudor times most families lived in the countryside

What can you remember?

1 Counties were divided into _____

2 What did the V brand stand for? _____

3 Did most families live in towns or the countryside? _____

4 What happened if there was a bad harvest? _____

Something to do

1 Draw your own picture of a Tudor village.

2 Describe the life of a poor person in Tudor times.

Travel

There were no cars or trains or aeroplanes or bicycles in Tudor times. They had not been invented. Towards the end of the period, wealthy people sometimes rode in coaches pulled by horses. Before that everyone travelled on foot or on horseback.

On land goods were **transported** in bags on horses or in carts. The easiest way to transport very heavy goods was by boat, using rivers or the sea.

Most of the roads were dreadful. Unlike modern ones, they did not have tar on them. They were just big paths through the countryside, sometimes very muddy and full of holes.

Travellers also had to be careful in case they were attacked by robbers.

Students on a country road near Oxford

Something to do

1 Draw a picture of a road near where you live, showing how it might have looked in Tudor times.

2 Make a list of the ways in which travelling in Tudor times was different from today. Why do you think journeys took much longer than they do today?

Plays and the theatre

The English language

Nowadays just about everyone living in England uses the same language – English.

It was not always like this. Before Tudor times:
- The Roman Catholic church used **Latin**, the language of the Romans.
- The law courts used French until the middle of the fourteenth century.
- English was not the same in different parts of the country. Most of us find **medieval** English almost impossible to understand.

By the reign of Queen Elizabeth I English was settling down and becoming quite like the language we use today.

One reason for this was the invention of **printing** – using a machine to copy words and pictures onto a page rather than doing it by hand. Printers wanted to use the same words and spellings for all their books.

*One of the first printing machines, or **presses***

The first plays

Plays began in medieval times. They were acted by groups of actors, or **players**, who travelled around from town to town. They acted in the open air, on carts or platforms in the town square or market place.

The plays were quite simple. They were either well-known stories from the Bible, or tales about right and wrong.

Theatres

In Elizabethan times plays became longer and more complicated. They were not just about religious matters, and they became more and more popular, especially in London.

Plays were performed in the courtyards of inns or in the halls of great houses. Towards the end of Elizabeth's reign, the first theatres were built. They were all in London.

From an Elizabethan picture of the Swan Theatre, 1596

Theatres were large wooden buildings with many sides. The stage was in the middle, sheltered from the sun and rain by a cover known as the 'heavens'. The audience either stood or sat on the ground around the stage, or paid for seats around the side of the theatre.

Audiences were not as polite as they are today – if they did not like a play they shouted and booed, like a crowd at a football match!

What can you remember?

Put a tick (✔) in the box if the sentence is correct:

1 There were theatres in medieval times. ☐

2 Elizabethan audiences were well behaved. ☐

3 The Roman Catholic church used the Latin language. ☐

4 Printing helped the English language settle down. ☐

5 Every town had its own theatre. ☐

William Shakespeare

Our greatest playwright

William Shakespeare, the greatest of all English **playwrights**, was born in Stratford-upon-Avon in 1564. When he grew up he moved to London to become an actor. He started writing plays and poems too.

William Shakespeare

Shakespeare knew exactly what his audiences liked, and he made sure that his plays had something for everyone. Some were very serious and sad, about kings and war and murder. Others, the **comedies**, were more light-hearted.

Shakespeare's plays were popular with all sorts of people, including Queen Elizabeth. She asked for special performances at court.

Shakespeare was so successful that he was able to retire to Stratford, where he died in 1616.

Something to do

1   Colour the picture of the Swan Theatre and label the following: stage, heavens, seats, actors. Explain how it is different from a modern theatre.

2   Find out the names of six of Shakespeare's plays. Have any of them been put on in a theatre near you?

Tudor architecture

Changing styles

There are many Tudor buildings still standing. They show us the different styles of Tudor architecture, and how they developed over the years.

These pictures show how the architecture of great houses changed:

Compton Wynyates, an early Tudor mansion

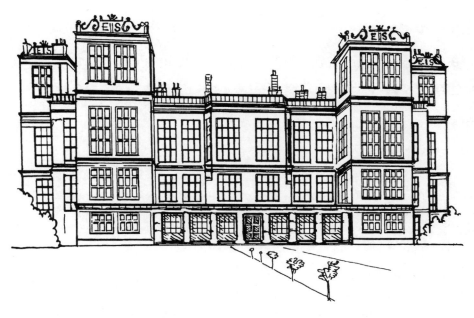

Hardwick Hall, built during the reign of Queen Elizabeth

Something to do

List the main differences between Compton Wynyates and Hardwick Hall. Look carefully at the shape of the *doors*, *windows*, and *chimneys*, the *decoration*, the *roofs* and the *pattern of the whole house*.

Ordinary Tudor houses

The best-known Tudor style is **half-timbered**, or black and white. The name comes from the black colour of the wooden frame and the white-painted material (usually brick) in between.

A half-timbered Tudor house

Something to do

What can we learn from Tudor houses about life in Tudor times? (Think about design, size, rooms, heating and cooking.)

Answers

Note: Children may need help with words in bold type.

Page 8: 1 = 1547, 2 = Tudor, 3 = Thomas Cromwell, 4 = Jane Seymour. Page 10: Correct sentences are – 2, 3, 4, 5. Page 11: 1 You might learn that people used unmechanised procedures, that they wore different clothes etc, 2 Six sources are books, letters, diaries, paintings, buildings and drawings. Page 12: 2 = 19th, 3 = 901, 1000, 4 = a 15th, b 16th. Page 14: 1 = ladies-in-waiting, 2 = court, 3 = privy chamber, 4 = chaplain. Page 17: 1 = Whitehall, St James's, 2 = hall, 3 = progresses, 4 = so that palaces might be cleaned, to be seen/to keep in touch, bored, 5 = quarters, 6 = four-poster. Page 20: Correct sentences are – 1, 4. Page 24: 1 = Bosworth, 2 = 1483-1485. Page 26: 1, 5, 6. Page 28: 2, 3, 5. Page 30: 1 = Armada, 2 = traded, 3 = invade. Page 33: 1 = voyages, 2 = missionaries, 3 = cargoes, 4 = era. Page 35: 1 = Spanish, 2 = Elizabeth I, 3 = Pacific, 4 = knight. Page 37: 1 = Virginia, 2 = Tower/prison, 3 = 1552-1618, 4 = James I. Page 40: 1 = population, 2 = imported, 3 = manufactured, 4 = merchants. Page 42: 1 = parishes, 2 = vagrant, 3 = countryside, 4 = starvation. Page 45: 3, 4.